IN THE LAND OF THE WAHOO TREES

poems by

Karen Mireau

Azalea Art Press
Sonoma · California

ISBN: 978-1-943471-86-7

Cover painting of Lake Cumberland
by Patti Edmon

*Dedicated to my friends, family,
and neighbors in Lexington, Kentucky,
and especially all the children
who have brought me so much joy.*

CONTENTS

Part II
Satori Organic Farm

PREFACE

Many marvelous and incredible things
defined my life in the fifteen+ years
I lived in Lexington, Kentucky.

There were children who filled my days
with their light and laughter and wisdom;
life-long friendships that evolved over time;
and creative opportunities that might
never have occurred elsewhere.

It was a time of profound joys,
but also one filled with tragedies
and heartbreaking sadnesses.

That these separate realities occurred
in a parallel space and time
is a mystery I continue to fathom.

IN THE LAND OF THE WAHOO TREES

PART I

BELL COURT

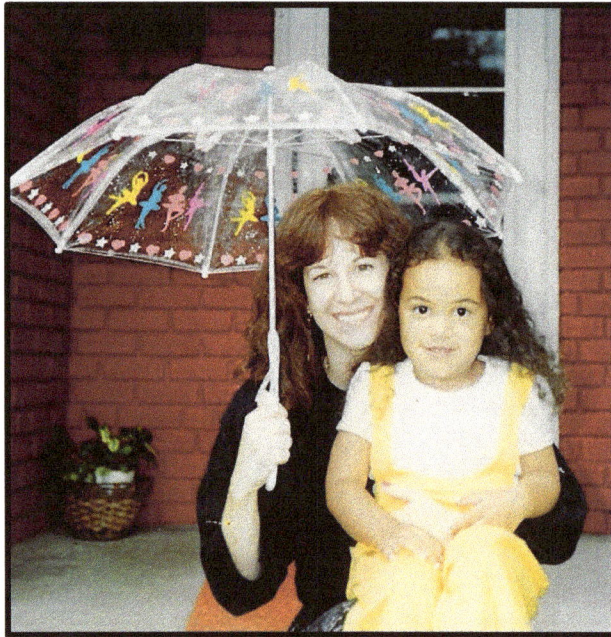

Karen & Marina | June, 1992
on Alma & George's Front Porch

MOUSE HOUSE

That summer we drove cross country,
Marina and I, our giant white rabbit "Bun Hun"
in the back seat of our sturdy Volvo sedan,
and we somehow made it through the desert,
the mountains and the plains in four days' time
before we crossed the border into Bluegrass land.

A charming duplex awaited us in Lexington
thanks to Patti, my childhood friend.
We had our clothes, some birthday toys —
(the week before, Marina had just turned four)
but that was it — we thought our things
would arrive the following week.

But never did. The moving van was stalled
somewhere in Washington state, and it would be
over a month before we'd have furniture
or anything that resembled a proper home.
Meanwhile, neighbors we hadn't even met
must have noticed our troubled state.

A card table and three chairs,
a box of dishes, a pot or two, some silverware,
showed up, like magic, on our front stoop.

Who these anonymous angels were, we never knew
but were a godsend to me, a single mother now
with a life pretty much in shambles.

Bell Court was a cozy neighborhood
in downtown Lexington, with a leafy park
and historic homes, each with a wide front porch.
In the late afternoons, elders called out
to the children and passersby to come up for
sweet tea or homemade lemonade and a chat.

The kids were free to play in the park
the adults keeping eye on them from afar—
an amazement to me coming from L.A.,
a place you'd never dream of letting your child
outside alone—there was always the danger there
of them being kidnapped right off the street.

It took a while to adjust to that. And Marina, too,
being the only multi-racial kid on the block—
who most in Kentucky would consider 'black.'
It had never occurred to me that the South
would be fifteen years or more behind
in honoring diversity but that, sadly, was a fact.

We got to know people after a spell
and when our things did finally arrive
it started to feel something like our home.
Except for one thing—the mice and rats
that had overtaken the basement's old dirt floor.
It took quite some doing to route them out.

I guess we did a small part in making our house
a local legend, for when it was complete,
the neighbors cheered—affectionately nicknaming it
the *Mouse House* (as you might easily predict).
To this day, though it's had several owners, I believe
folks on Boonesboro still refer to it that way.

The *Mouse House* | 2024

Patti & Jim | 1987

Karen& Patti | 2018

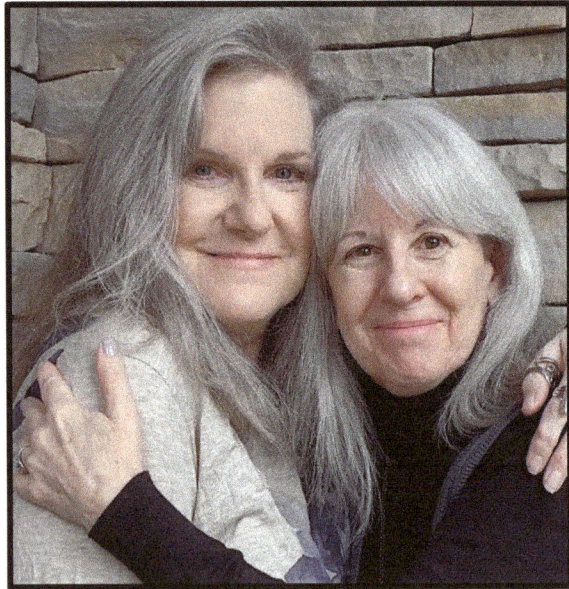

Patti & Karen | 2021

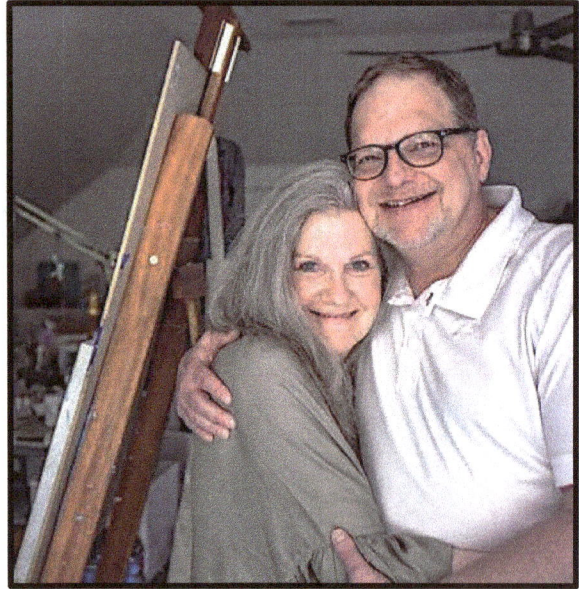

Patti & Jim | 2018

PATTI & JIM

From the time she was eleven, and I twelve,
Patti became my best and closest friend.
Living two doors down in Knickerbocker Hills,
we navigated our younger years through thick and thin
(and every other 'fine mess' in between)
though we lived in different states for most of it.

When she moved to Lexington a few years later
we visited each other several times a year,
and kept in touch by calls and writing letters
long before there were cell phones or social media.
Those were different times, to be sure,
but, it was a given—we kept on communicating.

I met Patti's soon-to-be husband, Jim,
when they first started dating—a perfect pair,
both artists and creative people, both funny as hell.
A few years later, after they married,
it was Patti who found the *Mouse House* for us
just around the corner on Boonesboro Ave.

To this day I marvel at how fate
brought me to live in Lexington once again —
the first time after a failed marriage,
working for a while at *The Bistro* in Chevy Chase
before I headed to a very different destiny
making cartoons in out west in La-La-Land.

The second, in 1992, after a decade
of marriage and another costly mistake
back to where I'd begun,
a single parent now
older, hopefully somewhat wiser,
but starting over nonetheless.

Once again, Patti and Jim were my lifeline.
To know Marina and I had a place to come to
and those we loved greet us with open arms
was a godsend of the finest kind, and to live again
near my dearest friends was as close to heaven
as anything I could have ever imagined.

To this day I'm ever and forever in their debt.

CLAIRE

On one of the first days at the *Mouse House*
I came home from *Kroger-ing* and there was a little girl
sketching pictures on our front porch with colored chalk.
She smiled, barely looking up at me. "I'm Claire,"
she announced, continuing to draw ever so dreamily,
"And you have a girl just my age, named Marina."

"Yes, that's true," I said.
Marina was next door with Alma and George.
She hadn't met any neighborhood kids yet,
so when she saw Claire, she was a bit reserved.
But it didn't last. They started drawing together
and before long they were the best of friends.

Claire lived just a few houses down from us
at the bend in the road on Delmar.
Big pine trees shadowed their front porch,
a perfect place in the summer heat
for kids to do crafts and spit watermelon seeds
on the patchy grass.

The *Mouse House* had a screened-in back porch
where the kids would play on rainy days,
singing, dancing, making animals of papier-mâché.

Claire and Marina had fun having sleepovers,
painting, and getting into whatever mischief they could.
They loved cartoons, and watched tons of those, too,

Her mom, Annie, and I got to be great friends
and though 'co-parenting' wasn't yet a thing
it's what we did right from the beginning—
sharing time for parents' nights out,
vacationing with the kids, when and where
all kinds of trouble might ensue.

Like the time with Annie that Marina and Claire
collected far too many rocks and in the middle of the lake
sunk their canoe. Or once, in New Hampshire,
when Claire took off her life vest, the two
got stuck down the lake in the rowboat, and my mother
(mad as a hornet) had to come to their rescue.

My favorite story has to do with when
we moved to Spurr Road on our farm, *Satori*.
We had just dug a pond and the yard was a disaster.
I begged Marina and Claire to stay cleaned up
before guests arrived for a birthday dinner.
You might imagine what happened next.

Yup. Mud Girls.
Covered from head to toe with icky-sticky goo.

You had to laugh. This was what the girls
would often do — find some funny way to bend the rules.
They were naughty rebels and trailblazers —
the very best you could imagine them to be.

We came to love Claire as a sister, a friend,
a dear daughter. Now both she and Marina
have two children of their own, each a boy and a girl.
There's no telling what will happen next.
As my mother once told me:
"I hope you have one just like you."

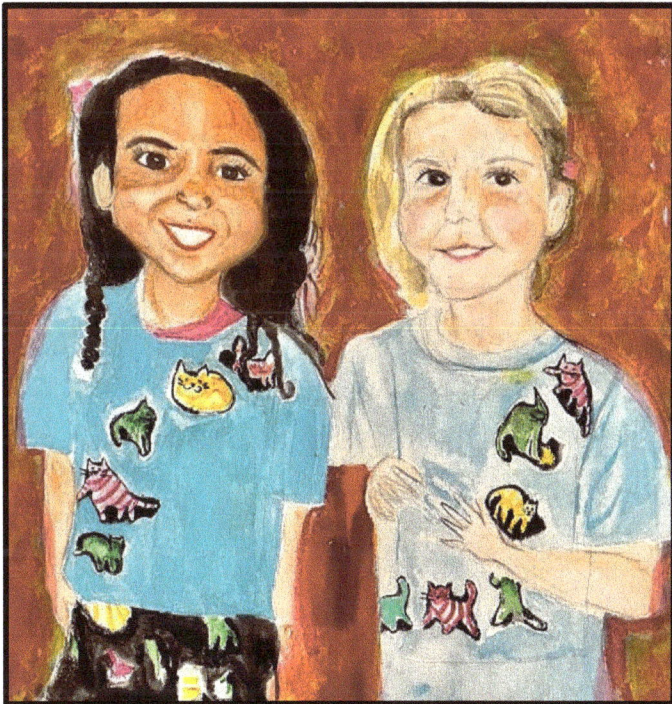

Marina & Claire | painting by Marina

Claire & Marina | "Mud Girls"

DORAFLEA

I couldn't blame her.
Marina missed her friends in L.A.
They'd all gone to preschool together —
and here she'd made only one new friend.
(That was, of course, the adorable, inimitable Claire.)
But still, my daughter was often lonely.

There wasn't much I could do,
but make an imaginary playmate for her.
She was put together with an old sheet
stuffed with cotton, straggly yarn for hair,
and mismatched button eyes. We dressed her
in some of Marina's outgrown pjs.

"Doraflea!" Marina called her at first sight.[1]
And she sat with us at every meal
with her own plate and fork and knife,
Marina reminding her of her manners:
"Elbows off the table, Doraflea," she'd say.
"Don't talk with your mouth full."

---

[1] Marina's favorite movie at the time was *The Wizard of Oz* and our Dorothy became "Doraflea."

Not to worry. Doraflea didn't say much,
just kept us company at that card table
day after day making us feel like a family.
I don't remember when it was,
but there came a time when our beloved Doraflea
was stowed away somewhere behind the winter coats.

Marina had more friends by then, me too
but I still think about Doraflea
and how much it meant to have her
sitting at our table, even if she *was* imaginary.
We had a lot of important conversations then
that to this day, I still remember fondly.

ALMA & GEORGE

Next door to us lived Alma and George
already in their early eighties then, I suppose.
Marina would wave to them shyly from the porch
and they would beckon her over. She'd smile, then hide.
One day, she bravely wandered up. And that was that.
It wasn't long before we adopted one another.

You couldn't knock on the door
at Alma and George's before they'd pull you in
and sit you down at their wooden kitchen table
for a full feast of her home cooking, or at the very least
a piece of her Apple cake and coffee —
you weren't allowed to leave 'til you were full.

George, he'd carve little toys of wood
and leave them in the crook of the water maple tree
for Marina to find "from the fairies."
He taught her how to tie her shoes
and ride a two-wheeler, among a million
other wonderful, loving, useful things.

The Johnsons became like grandparents —
they were that kindly and sweet.
From Eastern Kentucky, they'd never spent

much time with "colored people," they said.
But they fell in love with Marina
and told me "it changed their minds."

I never heard words so profound.
They already knew, of course, the sting of bias
especially towards those raised in poverty
and other such silly, ugly, stupid, superficial things.
They took in foster kids, more than a dozen
in their time, even well after they both retired.

Fed them, mended their clothes, taught them
right from wrong, lived a life of love and compassion.
And when Alma became sick and confined to her bed,
she'd shown us exactly what anyone of conscience
would need to do. It was my honor then, my blessing,
to tend to her the year before she died.

Every day they taught us the meaning
of ministering, of sacrifice, of giving up of self,
of how to make a difference, no matter how small,
how one-to-one, hand-to-hand, heart-to-heart,
sometimes people might change their thinking—
even if it was just a little at a time.

Alma & George
On Their Front Porch | 607 Boonesboro Avenue

PIANO MAN

for George Harlan Johnson
(1916-2012)

George's father died when he was eleven
and he went to work on the corner selling papers
to support his mother, sister, and two brothers.
He managed to finish eighth grade, though,
before he went to work full time in Louisville
in a woolen mill, where he also learned to sew.

When he was old enough, he joined the WPA
as a logger in the Civil Conservation Corp.
Then in 1938, at 21, he up and joined the Navy,
and traveled the world assigned to cargo ships
carrying freight engines between China,
the Philippines, and Central America.

He found he could fix almost anything,
could figure things out when others hadn't a clue.
Had an ear for things, too, could zero in
on problems with an engine long before it faltered.
He worked his way up, ran the engine rooms
until resigning in '58, a Chief Petty Officer.

After that, he wasn't sure what he'd do. He was only 42.
He talked his way into a job repairing piano parts.
Although he'd never played the piano in his life,
he found he could tune them like a pro.
And he did just that for 28 years all over the Midwest
and Kentucky, until he began losing his hearing.

When his first wife, Amy, died of cancer
George married her nurse, Alma Hurley, a bit of a scandal.
They stayed married fifty years after that. How'd they do it?
Alma said, "Everything we done, we done together."
George's only life regret? In his own words:
"Not smoking and drinking when I had the chance!"

George Johnson | 1938

THE ANGEL OF BELL COURT

for Alma Ann Hurley Johnson
(1918-2004)

She had a way with flowers
with all things green and growing.
She was magic with children
we were all hers, we heard her say.

With her brown eyes, kind and soft
with her cool palm at our cheek.
She felt the thread of our history
in every quilt she stitched.

With her we felt like continuing
like adding to and giving,
like planting something bright and wild
near the front porch swing.

How she loved her George
how she knew him so well,
and encouraged others to love him, too
when his generosity went unnoticed.

He rarely called attention to himself
always it was, *Alma, Alma.*
She marveled at his deep humanity,
found his stubbornness amusing.

All of us knew they were of one strength
George and Alma, Alma and George,
inseparable strands, reaching up
towards that shining place.

And they brought down their gifts
and handed them to us, one-by-one.
Because it meant everything to them
and because it was everything they had.

And Alma would smile that smile
and tilt her head,
looking like a young girl
in a meadow full of country flowers.

For she had a way with flowers
and knew that in her autumn
there would be rare seeds of many kinds
springing from season to season

Like hope from the new ground.

Alma & George's Home
607 Boonesboro Avenue

19

ODE TO ANNIE

We'd never known a woman
with so kind a heart—always offering
to lend a hand to any who needed help.
Never asking for validation for what surely
took her time and determination—
but that, in a nutshell, is our Annie.

Everything Annie does has a creative spin.
From crafting handbags, quilts, and clothes,
to making a mean white chicken chili—
she teaches us by patient example,
a natural educator of the finest sort,
all manifested with exquisite finesse.

How does she manage to do all this?
Minister to family and friends and run a house
and work full time while continuing to be
a good, devout Catholic who pays attention
to her neighbors as well as strangers in her midst?
It's clear. It's more than a calling—it's an art.

She's seriously funny as all get out.
I can hear her zany laughter to this day,
see her dark curly hair framing her sweet face

as she makes a joke or turns ABBA up loud
on the stereo so we can all drink wine, sing,
and dance together like lunatics in her living room.

There's few of us who'd measure up to her
but she'd never claim it that. "No, no," she'd humbly say
"it's just what you do to be a human being."
That's the thing with Annie—and so much more—
it's the beautiful, loving world she weaves around us
before our barely knowing it's been done.

Annie | 2021

RATTIGAN

This was something new.
There was a rustling sound in the closet
in Marina's room we hadn't before heard.
And soon it became clear:
there was *something* in there — and it *wasn't good*.
Again, we had to call the exterminator.

We shut the door and left the room
and soon the rustling got worse, combined
with the awful, incessant sound of *gnawing*.
Whatever it was, it was definitely not amused,
This we knew for sure — it was trying to chew its way out.
We saw its tooth marks on the door frame.

A man arrived at the front porch.
He had beady eyes, a wispy light-brown moustache,
and a twitchy air. (We looked for a tail, found none.)
He tapped a baseball bat nervously in his hand.
"Where's it at?" he asked. Then trotted up the stairs.
We heard a loud BANG. Then silence.

He came down swinging it by the tail.
The body was about eight inches long
with the tail even longer. I was horrified, Marina was sad.
"His name is 'Rattigan'," she said, "My dear old friend, Rattigan."
Apparently he'd been living in her room
far longer than I knew.

HANNAH & MIKAL

On the first day of school
just a few blocks from the *Mouse House*
Marina and I walked hand-in-hand
to Ashland Elementary.
A scary time for a five-year-old girl.
A wistful, lonely time for her Momma, too.

At the front door, the teachers stood and smiled
welcoming the new students,
but Marina and one other little girl hung back.
Not ready. Not ready just yet, for that.
The girl's mom introduced herself as Mikal,
and her daughter, as Hannah.

The girls looked each other over,
liked what they saw — there was a sweetness
in each of them that was palpable.
Hannah with her curly light-brown hair,
Marina with her long dark ringlets.
Two cutie pies if ever there were ones.

The final school bell rang. Time to go in.
Marina looked fearful. Hannah seemed
about to cry, or throw up, or both.

Mikal and I both had tears in our eyes
as Marina gently took Hannah's hand
and together they crossed the threshold.

Hannah Shafer & Marina Mendez
"Thing 1 and Thing 2" | Halloween 1999

THE STORY OF
MELISSA & ALISON

These two miraculous Banford girls!
Who knew we'd all be together for years
after their father asked me on an unlikely date?
But Ali and M'lissi, as we still call them,
were the perfect bait—Marina and I
fell in love with them instantly.

Sleepovers, drinking cocoa, watching cartoons,
eating *Mouse House* pancakes and bacon—
it all was a dream come true for Marina, who now
had two new sisters (along with dear, sweet Claire)
and oh, what a time we had, for years and years
long after their dad and I were through.

It wasn't any easy time for them growing up,
to be sure. Like the time Ali got suspended from school
for playfully dying her hair 'Wildcat Blue.'
Or the time they got locked out of their house
and had to break a window to get back in
after climbing up and over the two-story roof.

Not to mention the year they spent
at the Kentucky Horse Park
living at the local campground,
or studying martial arts, enduring
a turned-upside-down world
of their Sensei's own imagining.

Despite these challenges, they survived
and flourished — Ali as a social worker,
M'lissi as the gifted artist
we always knew she would become,
both as wives and mothers,
now with two children of their own.

What a treasure it was to see them grow
into such fine, creative beings.
They have given Marina and I
so much happiness and so many
beautiful, unforgettable memories.
We are so much in awe of each of them!

1996

Melissa Banford, Alison Banford,
Claire Barrett, Marina Mendez,
Hannah Shafer, & Mandy Williams
rollerblading up the driveway
at the wedding on Spurr Road
of Bill Smith and Karen Mendez

Melissa Banford, Marina Mendez,
Claire Barrett, Hannah Shafer,
& Alison Banford at the home of
Annie L'Esperance and Jerome Keeler
on Delmar Avenue

2018

MEADOW DAWN

She was a rare descendant of Atlantis,
a precious and ethereal will-o'-the-wisp of a girl
with hair the color of the sun, and eyes as blue
as a field of forget-me-nots, so filled
with love for everyone, you couldn't help
but love her too.

Before we even met, I knew she'd be
a beloved daughter, so when I saw her
at *The Atomic Cafe* that night across the room
I did a double take. I wasn't yet dating her father,
but when she walked up to greet him,
I instantly knew.

She'd appeared to me the night before
when her face appeared behind me in the mirror.
Smiling that mischievous Cheshire cat smile,
we had a telepathic conversation
(almost impossible to describe). But it was clear—
our lives would always be connected.

A year later we'd be living in the same house—
Marina, myself, Bill, and Meadow,
the middle child of his own three daughters.

When we married in Tennessee,
it was Meadow and Marina who stood up for us
as we officially became a family.

Meadow became the spiritual anchor
of the household, always seeing things
with deep intuition, and with an uncanny way
of knowing how things would unfold
even before they happened.
From the beginning, I admired her greatly.

Marina, now eight, worshipped her new big sister.
She shadowed Meadow—spying on her every move
even dressing like her before they went to school.
It annoyed teenage Meadow beyond belief
to have a little sister who wouldn't leave her be
even for a nano-second.

But they found their ways to get along—
practicing martial arts together,
and bouncing off the farmhouse walls,
sharing music, movies, and video games,
telling each other scary paranormal tales,
hiking together in the Red River Gorge.

Ten years later, when her dad and I parted
and I found myself some 3,000 miles away,
we stayed true to our beautiful bond.
When it came time to drive from Berkeley
to North Carolina to be with Marina and Zoey,
she was the one I wanted to come along.

We had a memorable stay in Big Sur
in the Van Gogh room at Deetjen's Inn,
then hit the hot springs at three a.m. at iconic Esalen.
With brilliant stars overhead, the crescendo
of turquoise surf below, the drummers softly began
as over the Santa Lucias rose the full moon.

It's something I'll never, ever forget.
I'll always be grateful for that magical moment,
and for Meadow, who came into my life
just as things were about to change forever—
and who stayed to become not only a daughter
but one of my most beloved best friends.

Marina, Meadow, Karen | Red River Gorge

Tracy, Marina, Meadow, Claire | 1996

Meadow & Marina | 1997

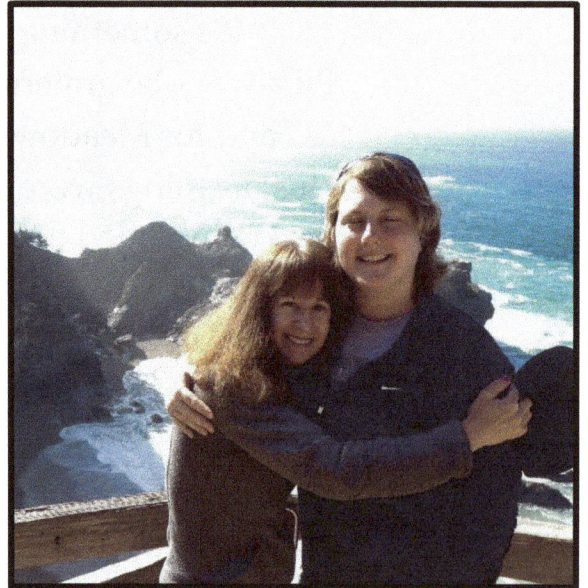

Meadow & Karen | Big Sur | 2013

TROUBLES

Marina and I had our troubles, that was certain.
How could anyone leave a million dollar house
for a yet-to-be-seen rental in central Kentucky?
But it was true—I happily left it all behind
just so my daughter and I could be safe
and have some peace of mind.

I knew if I'd stayed in L.A.,
I'd work three jobs to keep the status quo
(and never have time to be with my toddler girl).
I knew if I'd stayed, her father would haunt us
and that terror would get worse—
my four step-children there could attest to this.

So it was decided. I packed everything up
and we made the move. My divorce wouldn't clear
for many months—I later found he'd been in arrears
for the mortgage, back alimony, and child support—
a slick Hollywood trick to break the bank
and rob the house of equity.

It worked. We arrived in Kentucky stone broke.
It would be five years before things settled,
but I didn't care. I was free.

I had my own life back. I could start again.
Somehow here and there I found freelance work.
I managed to make ends meet. Just barely, though.

Until one day, Marina came to me, saying:
"Mom, what does every kid have in common?"
I was busy washing dishes. I said, "I don't know . . ."
"Trouble," she said, spelling it T-R-U-B-B-L-E.
My jaw did a cartoon drop. She was so right.
It was universal to every single kid we knew.

She started working on her idea right away,
excitedly drawing the cat and characters
based on all her old friends from Sierra Madre—
(and herself as the star of the show.)
"What a great cartoon it'll be!" Marina said.
With a few story ideas in hand, we were ready to go.

Trubbles showed how kids got into trouble
but also ways they could get out of it—
by asking for help, telling the truth,
making amends. It all made perfect sense.
I sold some first edition books
and bought us tickets to New York City.

The next day, with a one typewritten sheet
and artwork that Marina, Ali and M'lissi
had done the night before, it was presented
to a producer at Children's Television Workshop,[2]
who got the idea and bought the concept
then and there. Something unheard of to this day!

Marina as a Cartoon Character

---

[2] Nina Elias Bamberger (1954-2002), was the Executive Producer at Children's Television Workshop (now Sesame Workshop) who oversaw production of Jim Henson's *Big Bag Series*. *Troubles the Cat* was one of seven animated shorts, one of only two that aired in the 2nd season.

Renamed *Troubles the Cat,* on June 2, 1996,
Marina's show premiered on Cartoon Network
in 47 countries, making her that year
the only female independent U.S. cartoon creator
and the first multi-racial child to originate
(and star) in her own animated show.

Marina's old and new friends now could plainly see
you could take something from your imagination
and make it real. How lucky were we?
We even had our five minutes of celebrity!
All because we'd had some rather tough luck—
and refused to let it get the better of us.

DON PRATT

On the northeast corner of Walton
at the end of Boonesboro Avenue
was the Woodland Grocery
owned by the infamous Don Pratt

That was where
all the Lexington literati gathered
to shoot the shit and hash out
the political news of the day.

I was terrified to go in there
even for something I might need because —
and this may sound silly — it was always
filled with very intense men.

When walking in, I felt like
all eyes were upon me, not just because
I was a New Yorker, newly arrived
from California (heaven forbid).

But a writer who was curious
about their conversations and convictions,
not just there for a ham sandwich
(which were delicious, by the way).

True, I was a fish out of water
and no one knew what to make of me
except for Don, who was always kind
and a gentleman—I could tell he saw me.

Always making me feel welcome
and the more I learned about him
the more I liked his rabble-rousing
out-of-the-ordinary ways.

First off, he was lifelong friends
with Alma and George—I'd heard
he'd been in George's boy scout troop
where some kind of trouble had ensued.

But he and George patched things up
and, perhaps inspired by the life they led
tending to those who were challenged
Don began taking in foster children, too.

Eventually 65 of them, adopting two—
many of them victims of abuse,
and even though he was single,
the first in the state to take in non-related girls.

This I witnessed: him bringing
the kids' clothes for Alma to mend
and getting advice on everything
that had to do with raising them.

Later, he started gathering suitcases
and donating them to foster agencies
so that the kids wouldn't suffer the indignity
of moving with their things in garbage bags.

This, I thought, was a remarkable act
but Don, I came to find, had a knack
for running against the status quo
and focusing on the true heart of things.

An activist and advocate all his life
for anti-bias and social change,
(I love that the newspaper considered him
"an agitator in residence.")

He'd marched and protested
with Dr. Martin Luther King
dedicating himself to nonviolence
and eradicating "polite racism" in Lexington.

Going to federal prison in 1968
for two years for resisting the draft
though he was exempt from service
for a certifiable medical condition.

But I didn't know all that then—
I only knew the Don I met at the Johnsons
or the grocery, or walking down the street,
from time to time swapping tales.

I didn't know that his moral convictions
and grassroots efforts, along with others,
saved the Red River Gorge from being
turned into a lake and sure oblivion.

Or that his citizenship and conscience
were celebrated by Wendell Berry
in a chapter in *The Longlegged House,*
Berry's very first book of essays.

What I came to admire beyond anything else
was Don's fearlessness and sense of justice,
his ability to bring people together
and start a spirited dialogue.

As he once said:
"I live every chance I get
to do something good" — that's just one reason
my life will always be inspired by Don Pratt.

Don Pratt | inside the Woodland Grocery | 1980
Photo by Christy Porter

I gave my entire soul to a garden once.

That in itself is not unusual,
but what happened next sparked an odyssey
that took twenty-four years
to fully comprehend.

The following writings are my testament
to our ability to heal from trauma —
and to find beauty and grace and truth
in the telling of one's story, no matter
how difficult that may be.

PART TWO

SATORI ORGANIC FARM

One afternoon I came home to my farm in Lexington, Kentucky, to find my then-husband, who was a holistic healer, in an intimate situation with one of his patients. It was soon discovered that for many years he had been an unrepentant predator of both young and elderly women, and that he had many such "interactions" with his clients.

In that one moment, everything I had worked so hard to build for over a decade was instantly shattered and ripped away. As is common with betrayal, those that did know about his deceptions never said a word to me . . . until later . . . when the facts began to emerge and become known to our community. Then confessions began pouring forth from family, friends, and the people my husband and I had tended.

Everywhere I went, someone would approach me and tell me a story of how they'd been lured into a relationship with my soon-to-be ex-husband. Some wept out of shame or embarrassment. Many expressed how they thought we had been "the perfect couple" and so never suspected that they were being groomed for abuse.

This, to me, was more shocking and traumatizing than the discovery of the affairs themselves. I felt horribly sad for the people who had been victimized. I felt at fault for not having recognized that these crimes (and I do believe that they were criminal acts) were transpiring in my own home. Mostly, I felt sorry for myself and my children. The private shame I felt was unspeakable and immense.

Life for me in Lexington, which was really more like a small town at that time, became unbearable. The trauma was so intense that within a month's time I put my farm up for sale and held a spiritual clearing ceremony to rid the land, the house, and the barn of any residual bad energies. With lots of help, I held a series of barn sales in the freezing cold. Then, when spring arrived, I packed up everything and moved across the country to Berkeley, California — a place I had been only once, and where I knew no one. My grief was that deep and that great.

To say that I missed being so far away from my daughter, my adopted spiritual children, and the friends who for over a decade had become my chosen family is a terrible understatement. Equally tragic was the loss of my garden. There, in that perfect matrix of earth and air and sweet spring water, my life — my real connection to Kentucky — had begun. And it was there, under an ancient apple tree just coming into leaf, that I cried my most bitter, heart-broken tears when it ended.

Farmhouse & Raised Bed Garden | Spurr Road | Lexington | 2002

It was a series of gardens, actually, that became an organic permaculture farm loosely following the philosophies of Rudolph Steiner. One morning, on what had been a patch of ragged grass surrounding our 100-year-old farmhouse, I peeled back the sod to reveal a riverbed of solid clay. It was decided: raised bed gardens it would have to be. And so I began to construct drystone walls with milky-green, hand-hewn Indiana limestone hauled up from the remains of an deserted half-buried foundation down the road.

Satori Farm Potager Garden | First Year | 2000
View from Marina's Window

Before long, the enclosures were filled with earth and compost and the long-anticipated magic of planting began. One 60' x 60' garden, in French potager style, had crushed stone paths that surrounded a center overflowing with French Lavender and antique white Iris. In the surrounding beds, I planted an eclectic mix of heritage fruits, vegetables and edible flowers, including forty kinds of garlic.

My daughter Marina's bedroom window looked out over this garden, and I filled it with changing colors and textures that I thought she might find interesting. She was, and continues to be, an artist. It was always my secret hope that she might remember this garden later in life, and derive some inspiration from it.

The Angel Garden

A second garden hugged both sides of a pathway built from the drive to the front door of the house. Here was my "Angel Garden," filled with starts and bulbs that friends and family placed (often anonymously) on my front porch. In a season's time, there was a rainbow of Alliums, Columbine, Snowbells, purple and apricot Irises, Lilies of all description, and many plants that had passed, hand-to-hand, through generations to now call my Angel Garden home.

I named the farm (prophetically, ironically), *Satori* — Japanese for 'instant awakening.' As it grew, three orchards were planted with saplings grafted from stock indigenous to the area, many varieties dating back to the 1800s. Apples, apricots, peaches, pears, nectarines, grapes, and berries of all kinds flourished. A water garden began to take shape near the pond and 10-foot berms lining the perimeter of the property, also made of earth and compost, became vertical gardens of ancient grains such as wheat and amaranth, and medicinal herbs.

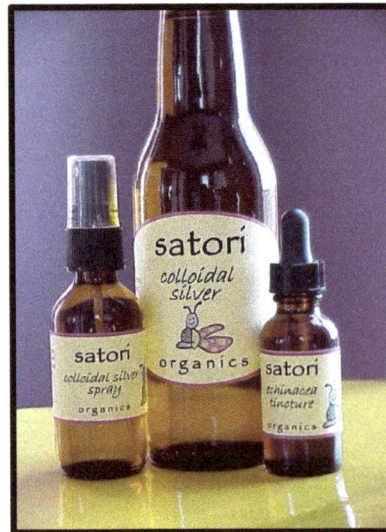

Satori Medicinals

Many other medicinal plants, such as Burdock, Chicory, Comfrey, Nettle, Plantain, Pokeweed, and Sumac grew at the edges of the farm. These were wildcrafted and, like those we grew, were made into healing poultices, infusions, decoctions, and tinctures.

The five-acre farm was set at the top of a hill in the middle of thoroughbred horse breeding farms that extended as far as the eye could see. It was all that remained of the original 3,000-acre parcel dating to the early 1800s. The house itself was a five-bedroom circa 1900 Craftsman-style bungalow with a wide front porch and a porte cochere. (The plans, I learned, had originally been ordered from a Sears catalog.) Behind the house was a 2,000-square foot "five-bent" tobacco barn, which was slowly being converted into a healing center.

The Farmhouse

The Barn at Sunset

The land the farm sat on had an interesting topography. Below it were miles and miles of shale and limestone caverns that radiated out from the center of the hill like the spokes of a wheel. In several places near the farm were sinkholes where just a few meters below you could see groundwater in these caverns rushing on its way to join the Kentucky River. The presence of moving underground water, and the chakra-like formation the farm sat upon, made it energetically very unique.

The water was an inspiration. We dug two wells, and laid a geothermal loop underneath a 1/2 acre pond which kept the house an even 55 degrees, even in winter.

Mallards on the Pond in Spring

Two windmills provided all the power we needed to the barn—all with the aim of eventually becoming completely "off grid" and energy sustainable. Plans to include solar power were in the works. We were fairly close to attaining that goal.

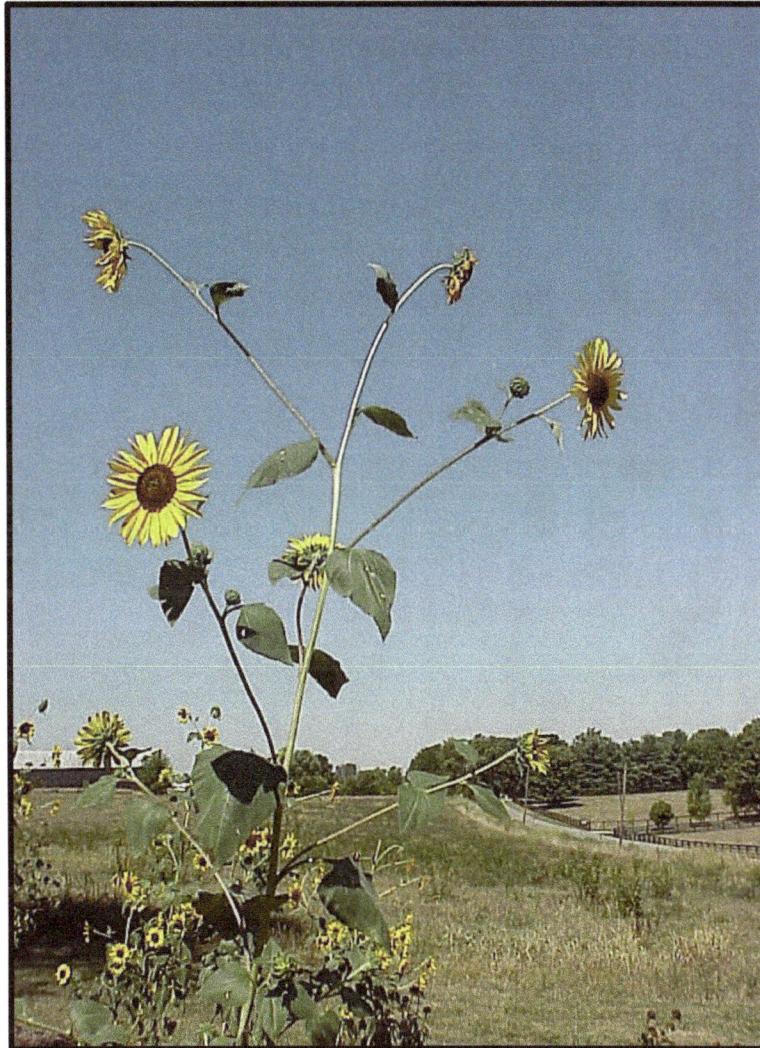

Volunteer Sunflowers at Satori

Despite what was going on behind the scenes, there was a sense of what I can only describe as "rightness" that settled over the farm. It did indeed become a healing center where cancer patients, many broken beyond repair, came seeking one last solution, a cure yet untried. Some regained their health, others did not; but the farm existed as a beacon of hope for those who had already exhausted both traditional and alternative medical efforts as well as their financial resources. Some paid us in food from their own farms; others bartered for care with their services. Although on paper we were what you might consider 'poor,' that cash-less system worked well for everyone.

We flew under the radar. Even acupuncture, well-accepted elsewhere in the country, was considered a radical treatment in Kentucky at that time and was illegal.

Heritage Snowdrops

Ancient Wheat

The traditional medical community in Lexington soon closed ranks against what they imagined was a threat to their livelihood. Friends who were using complementary medicine modalities were forced to close their practices. They, too, had to go underground.

We raised all our own food on the farm, from ancient grains to many heritage varieties of fruits and vegetables. It was grown not as produce for sale, but as medicine for the body, for the soul, for the aching spirit. These were given freely as treatments and as gifts to the people who came there.

In the end, this good, well-intentioned work was negated by the unethical actions of my husband once they were revealed. But at the time very few around us (other than the victims) suspected that he lived a double, carefully hidden life.

When I made my final goodbye, it was not just to my farm, but to that soulful way of life, the one that existed outside of my husband's actions. In tending it, the farm had been a profound inspiration; and it had also been my teacher, my solace. I sensed that I might never fully recover from what had happened there, but some inner wisdom told me that forgiveness was essential for me to go on living my life with any kind of peacefulness.

"To forgive, but never to forget"—was the conscious choice I made at the time. I have never regretted it.[3]

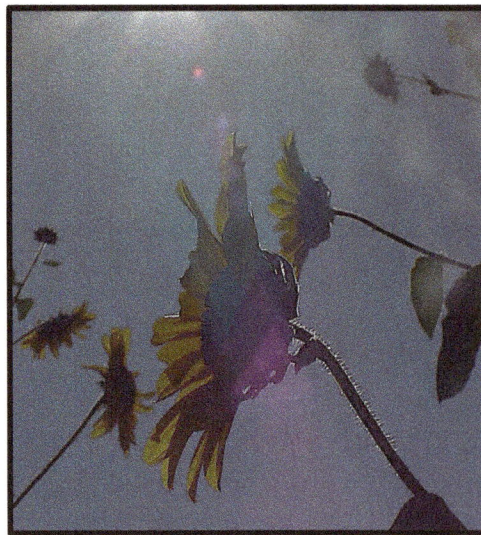

Antique Sunflowers

---

[3] Billy Johnson Smith (BJ) suffered from a variety of addictions before his death in 2023, at age 73, from Parkinson's Disease. For more about Satori Organic Farm, please see the writings in *The Architect of Fire* (Azalea Art Press, 2024).

It took several years before I dared plant a garden again. This garden was on a steep hillside above the sea in the North Berkeley hills. The motivation for building it was in fact a gift from a lover who thought it might be good for me to put my hands back into the earth.

Once again, I found myself constructing walls and raised beds from scavenged, reclaimed stones. I didn't realize what an emotional experience this would be, how much grieving for my old garden still remained. To build something with someone, to put down roots again—all of this was terrifying. The deep wound within me reopened, and out poured a torrent of painful, important truths.

Once again, my garden became my teacher. As it took shape, my heart softened. The bond that developed between my friend and I as we pulled ivy, levered out old rocks, and planted vegetables, flowers, and herbs, felt strange and uncomfortable at first. Could I ever forgive myself for having been so gullible? Could I trust someone again? Could I truly give myself to another? Over time, in great measure because of witnessing my friend's own soulful relationship to the earth, my resistance to letting go (and letting in) allowed me this. It transformed me yet again.

When that relationship also ended in betrayal, it took me many years and a compassionate witness, my trauma therapist and now dear friend, Jennie Rose, to process and understand the source of so much sadness. Although it was many years before I found another place to set down roots, this much I believe even more fervently now: nothing we experience is ever wasted.

I gave my whole soul to a garden once; and, I am happy to say, I have been blessed with the chance to do it everywhere I have lived since. A garden, like the books we write, the art we create, is a sacred space of possibility and responsibility and healing. No matter what transpires, it is the rich loam from which the future flowers of life can — and will — grow. I continue to learn from that lesson every day.

It doesn't get much better, or more amazing, than that.

—Karen Mireau, July, 2024
originally written in 2010

Karen Mireau
"Queen of the Mulch Pile"
Satori Farm | 2000

EVERYTHING YOU NEED
IS HERE

It was early spring, and I was walking
somewhat aimlessly and despondently that day
as I sometimes did, around the perimeter
of the old farm I'd once lived upon,
when I came across some unusual stones.
They were sage green in color, lightly striated —
ones I'd never seen before.

Upon closer inspection, they must have been
part of a foundation of an old farmhouse.
This was clear, because there were irises
and other green shoots emerging here and there
from someone's long-ago, gone-to-seed garden.
As I dug around with a sharp stick, the stones
I saw, were laid in perpendicular rows.

Though eroded, they were squared blocks
and as I followed the lines of the foundation
it was apparent that the house was sited perfectly
to catch the sun or perhaps also the moon
in our part of the world —
that the trees surrounding it, though overgrown,
were well planned for shade and protection.

I'd been dreaming of a garden
at my new farm, but didn't have the resources
to build the raised beds I imagined.
It was then that I heard the voice,
loud as thunder, resounding through the woods,
and ringing — clear as a thousand bells — in my head.

It said:

EVERYTHING YOU NEED IS HERE

I fell back, in shock, in disbelief,
sat down on one of the old stones,
then heard it once again —
the intent this time went beyond mere words.
The message, so crystalline, was that everything
and anything we dream can be made real
if only we are open to seeing what is here before us.

Was it some god or goddess talking?
How could anyone argue with that?
I brought my banged-up 'barrow,
lifted out the old stones and wheeled them
to my farm, load by load, up the steep hill
where I laid them out on the grass.

A master stonemason happened by.
"Wow!" he exclaimed, "What ya got here
is some really nice Indiana Limestone!
Sure enough, that's what it is,
and if ya'd paid to have it quarried
and hauled to this site," he said,
"it'd cost ya twenty grand or more, for sure."

So go figure.
If I hadn't been depressed that day
and wended my way through that wood,
I would never have stumbled upon those stones
or heard that voice,
and my raised bed garden
would never have been built.

It was hard work.
Those blocks weighed 50-100 pounds or more.
I had to lift them with levers onto old sheets
and drag them where they'd be put into place.
It took me the better part of three weeks
to lay the stone, fill the enclosures with compost
and soil, and to line the circular path
inside the walls with white gravel.

When it was done, there was only one piece
left over — a gravestone for an infant.
No name, just the dates, 1802-1803.
And when I saw it I wept a tsunami of tears
like you would not believe — for that child,
whose life was so very brief,
for the woman who birthed it,
for the family who must have mourned it.

I cried.
For the sweet honesty of it
gracing my garden — that tangible marker of life,
of love, of loss, of birth, and death —
everything we crave or need or desire
or will ever experience here
together on this crazed, ephemeral earth.

THERE COMES A TIME

When we long
for a secret house
made of earth or leaves
a place to shelter from the rains
our sweet miseries bring

And we start the journey
casting everything aside
not knowing, once more
who we are
or who we were

or where we'll go
from here

THE BETRAYAL

When it was learned
abruptly — that our entire life
as husband and wife was fiction
that every word you spoke
every kiss you metered out
everything you did was a sham

The children, fortunately,
were mostly grown and gone.
Once the sad inventory of our life
all those objects we thought were so precious
were sorted, discarded, or given away —
before that final *au revoir*

What would remain?
but a few fading photographs
to remind us of the orchards we'd planted
the now maturing fruits falling
in the receding dusk
with no one left to harvest them

It all came down to this:
a dream manifested
through persistence and sheer toil
but a life, it must be also said
often filled with simple joys
and, sometimes, perfect silences

Therein lies the sadness —
for each of us awaits down the road
for whatever time may be left us
a grieving that seems an endless abyss
for what our life might have been
had it been real

and the relentless memory
of that first, ill-fated kiss

THE BEFORE

There were signs—
small ones at first
then others, more audacious
so over the top
that you or I or anyone else might
easily discard them as pure fantasy

Was it possible
to be deceived so boldly?
could someone you love be so calculating,
so manipulative, so evil?
it was so much better
not to know

So much better not to ask
when of course deep inside
every intuition screamed the question
every small betrayal confirmed
what you and everyone else already knew
was the honest answer

SPRING AGAIN

There was rain
and more rain
and spring
or something like it

You felt as if
you'd been shoved
face down into a ditch—
a thick Carhartt boot
planted squarely on your neck
your mouth stuffed silent
with grief and wet grit
so horrible, yet in some ways
tasting so sweet

And the flowers—*my oh my*
they all looked so different then
there were no more questions
no more answers
nothing more
that could possibly hurt you
yes, yes
it was pretty much
all up from there

BLACK MARKS

The way rain blown by the spring storm
slashes across the red oak planks
of the tobacco barn, branding
the thirsty wood with dark exclamations
seems an unmerciful accounting—
so many things were unexpected
so many things took a turn for the worse

There was a message in every shadow
every dark lie, every disturbing conundrum
even so, the clues constantly eluded me
(though quite possibly I wished that to be so).
Then, just when all seemed hopeless,
that too much was stacked against me,
the end game impossibly lost

this bitter, particular truth—
hidden for so long
so necessary now for my survival
emerges from the wet grain

WHAT MY LIFE HAS BEEN

A joysong
a surprising sorrow
tumultuous
a river deep
a strange wood
without end, a path
through magical hollows
that comes
to the edge of a cliff

Where I stand
over and over
about to jump
and then I do jump
(or not, either way)
suddenly I am on the other side
breathing fast
amazed at the breadth
of the chasm
behind me

A SONG
FROM UNKNOWN SOURCES

This is really the song
of an invisible bird
translated for your own enjoyment

The song goes like this:

life is, life is
it is, is, is
just what it is

Then the rain —
that blinding-knife-edged-Bluegrass rain
comes thundering down

IN THE LAND
OF THE WAHOO TREES

When the mockingbirds go temporarily mute
and the fading southern light conspires to lure me
into a meditative state, I await the fissured dusk
when the Wahoo's bark turns by degrees the color
of Maker's Mark, entangled with emerging starlight.
Here, in the advancing winter gloom —
such sights and simple joys are no small thing.

Of the bittersweet family
its purple bi-sexual flowers arrive in June —
a magnet for bees — its finely-serrated elliptical leaves —
home for moths and larvae of wide variety,
particularly that of the butterfly, 'Holly Blue,'
a favorite, too, of our common robin
so also known as *Robins' Bread.*

It appears in dappled sun
on moist rich Kentucky limestone soil —
called *Burning Bush* for its crimson foliage,
biblically ablaze in fall, or, my favorite appellation
Hearts Bursting with Love
for its four-lobed, roseate fruits beloved by birds
who generously spread its scarlet seeds about.

Early Colonists called it *Spindle-*
or *Skewer-wood,* perfect for crafting pipe, peg,
bobbin, or birdcage from each limber branch.
Named by the Dakota tribe
Wanhu or *Arrow Wood*
for its straight, sturdy stems
perfect for bows and shafts.

Boiled in water, its burnt umber seeds
yielded a yellow dye, or combined
with alum, a greenish hue, while oil
from the entire plant used for making soap.
The young shoots, fired and ground,
made a fine artists' charcoal,
also an essential ingredient of gunpowder.

Its dried root bark was widely praised
as a general tonic. A sprig of its leaves believed
to give protection from the plague
yet all parts of the plant are deemed medicinal—
its seeds an emetic and purgative, also insecticide,
parasiticide, diuretic, stimulant for heart, liver,
and even a cure for malaria.

Self-sowing, easily propagated by rhizome,
the Wahoo now considered an invasive pest
throughout the South and Midwest—*invasive*—
and yet a species people happily cultivate
to the demise of other native plants. Why?
My guess would be the jewel-bright leaves
that ignite the damp, drear wintry landscape.

The Wahoo's offer of hope
and visual relief is something I pray to find
when alone with my regrets, my hidden griefs
I await the mockingbird's return
to shake me from my sullen winter reverie
and remind me that no matter how deep our despair
might be — the marvelous does indeed exist.

AUJOURD'HUI

for the blackbirds
at Satori Farm, Lexington, Kentucky

Hope, have hope

This, the redwing blackbirds
constantly remind me—
with or without us
the ghost ocean of dawn will return

Thickening the hollows
erasing the hills' blue outline
rearranging the charcoal edges of the fields
to render a far more ethereal world

Hope, have hope

This is something
I might never have taken to heart
or would ever have imagined but for
the blackbirds' faithful pronouncements

One of a thousand reasons you and I
are tethered to this particular patch of earth—
here, where in each and every lifting darkness
the stuff of new dreams is being birthed

THE SLEEPING PORCH

In the last Kentucky light
the Wahoo trees turn the burnished hues
of tobacco, spilt bourbon, and reddened earth.
Their leaves jangle in the breeze
rusted violet : rubbed silver : milkglass green
jewels rarely named by you or me.

On the sleeping porch a young girl
inhales the almost solid summer heat
not at all surprised
when a halo appears
around the August Strawberry moon —
a kaleidoscope that alters everything.

Just beyond the screen door
a yearling nackers restlessly, wild-eyed
motioning for her to follow —
she grabs hold of its mane, and soon
over stone walls, shorn hedgerows
and aubergine pastures they fly

Past hemp barns, steel silos, gathering speed,
the fenceposts marking minutes
to the clickity-clack metronome of dreams.
Until night snaps shut, the moon disappears,
and the yearling fades into the velvet fields.
As if on cue night birds begin to sing.

This is what it means, she knows
to have a poet's heart—
even before opening her eyes
she begins to translate what she's seen,
as she does, has always done
each and every morning, afterwards.

PILEATED

Woodpeckers are desperately shy,
and more so the Pileated kind, they hide
from human contact, but by and by
if you are really lucky you'll get to see one
inadvertently in some remote stretch of forest
or happen upon one, nearby, by surprise.

This time was different—my friend Ann and I
were hiking one morning in Raven's Run
when something quite peculiar occurred—
as we were walking along the edge of the river
a female kept following us, from time to time
sounding out its signature chattering.

We were keeping to the meandering trail
but somehow it echoed the woodpecker's path
until we came to a small spring to rest, and looking up
saw that we'd been led to exactly where
the woodpecker was, quite high up a tree,
feeding her multiple offspring.

This was quite shocking, to be sure,
a Pileated mother showing us her nest
was something we'd never imagined seeing.
We watched her for quite some time
feed her young in complete peace and safety
in total awe of nature's mysterious intimacy.

Between us it became a running theme —
that a wild bird could trust our spirits so much
that she'd allow us to witness her vulnerability.
How could anyone ever discount that?
Forever after, neither of us, I believe
would ever find a walk in the wood quite the same.

**Karen
& Ann Bowe Barr | 2018**

THE LAST WAHOO

Wahoo!
An appropriate expression
when one sees unusual beauty
for the first time

When I first saw *Euonymus atropurpurea*
that early winter afternoon
its delicate apparition was something
not entirely comprehended or understood.

Still, it gave me pregnant pause
to consider how often we happen upon
such odd moments of wonderment—
if only we can manage to stay open to them.

When I left Kentucky a decade later
I knew I might never see a Wahoo tree again,
might never walk a wood where
its impossible beauty would take me by surprise.

To stir my faith in the infinite perfection
of this—our beloved Earth's dazzling design—
and that alone has been enough to strike me dumb
and keep me to this day, most happily in awe.

WAHOO!

ACKNOWLEDGMENTS

There are people
in the Land of the Wahoo Trees
whom I will never, ever forget.

And there are those
who may not ever know
how deeply they impacted my life.

Here, in alphabetical order
are many, though not all,
of those very special people.

Melissa Banford
& Alison Banford-Tighe

my first soul daughters in Lexington
and sisters to my daughter, Marina,
they are connected to us for life.

Ann Barr

supported me through many
difficult times and always inspires me
with her love of life and nature.

Claire Barrett

drew chalk pictures on our front porch
and immediately became family
on our first meeting at the *Mouse House*.

Malcolm Barrett

as father to Claire Barrett, Malcolm
has always been a significant part
of our life on Bell Court and elsewhere.

Kellie, John, Tristan
& Claire Considine

my neighbors two doors down were always
such sweet support to myself and Marina —
their kindness will always be remembered.

Patti & Jim Edmon

my best friends of over 50 years
who first brought me to Lexington, Kentucky
have never let me forget that I have a home here.

Alma & George Johnson

my adopted grandparents, mentors,
and next door neighbors on Boonesboro Avenue
taught me more than I can ever give them credit.

Betsy Johnson

the daughter of George Johnson
and her three daughters continue to be
beloved, trusted, lifelong friends.

Jimmy Johnson

the late son of George Johnson,
Jimmy and his family have always been
a beautiful part of our life on Boonesboro Avenue.

Annie L'Esperance
& Jerome Keeler

as they have always done, these dear friends
lovingly parent my children and grandchildren
as if they were their very own.

Don Pratt

Don's kindness to children,
and his generous spirit are all things
that will always inspire me.

Mikal & Hannah Shafer

spiritual sisters and special friends—
there is no way to describe my deep love
for these two beautiful souls.

Meadow Dawn Smith

she appeared in a vision,
and even before we met, she became
not only a sister to Marina, but
a daughter and a lifelong friend.

Tracy Belle Smith

forever linked to me as a daughter
and as a sister to Meadow and Marina,
Tracy is a creative light like no other.

The abstract painting on this book cover
is of *Patti's Cove* on Lake Cumberland.

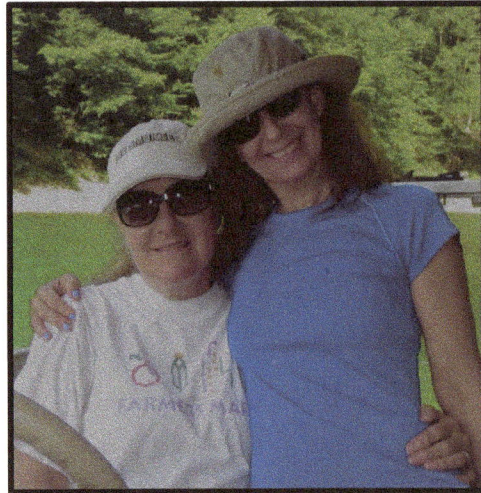

Patti Edmon & Karen Mireau
'Taking the Waters' | 2016

It is a place that exists as a source
of peace, inspiration, and happiness
for both the artist and the author.

*A special thank you to all my friends
& Bell Court neighbors, who made our life
in Lexington feel like a real home.*

You know who you are . . .

*I am overflowing with awe & love
for my beautiful daughter, Marina Leigh,
whose kindness & creativity
are always an inspiration to me.*

*My thanks also to artist Patti Edmon,
my lifelong friend, whose painting
of a magical cove at Lake Cumberland
graces the covers of this book.*

*My ongoing appreciation also goes
to my beloved friend, Jennie Rose,
for reparenting me & guiding me
to a place of peace & forgiveness.*

And last, but never least . . .

*My deep gratitude to my husband,
Raymond Jaye Rimmer,
who lends me strength when I need it most.
This book would not exist without him.*

ABOUT THE AUTHOR

Karen Mireau, 2023

Karen Mireau began her professional journey as a full-time poet. She soon discovered that this sensibility lent itself perfectly to the medium of film. In Los Angeles, after working as executive assistant to NBC CEO Grant Tinker and President Brandon Tartikoff, she co-founded an animation company that created **"Kissyfur"** and **"Foofur"**, two hit Saturday morning shows for **NBC,** and many concepts for toys, books, television, and film production.

She also found a distinct flair and passion for marketing. From merchandising and promoting her own TV shows she learned the principles of bringing complex concepts successfully to their target audience.

In her early thirties, Karen had the honor and wonder of birthing a beautiful, talented daughter, Marina Leigh Mendez Williams, and helping raise an extended family of marvelous and wildly creative sons and daughters, all of whom she adores dearly to this day.

During that time, she also developed *Satori*, a permaculture farm and healing center in Kentucky, based on the teachings of Rudolph Steiner, where she continued her life-long commitment as a self-avowed "Agricultural Anarchist" and "Entre-manure."

Karen continued her passion for marketing and children's media, resulting in **"Troubles the Cat,"** created with her daughter, Marina Mendez (now Williams), then 5 1/2 years old. "Troubles" premiered on **Cartoon Network** in 47 countries in **Jim Henson's** series **"Big Bag"** and was produced by **Children's Television Workshop**, of **Sesame Street** fame, and is currently being developed as a half-hour series with the original producer, internationally-renowned animator and film maker **R.O. Blechman**.

Troubles led to a natural expansion of her focus to nurture other authors, illustrators and creators of children's books, television and film. In her role as a "Literary Midwife" and founder of **Koo Koo & Company**, Karen traveled throughout the U.S. and Europe presenting children's media concepts to major publishers and distributors and launching many careers.

In 2008, Karen discovered a new direction in the form of helping others express and put their stories into print, and created **Azalea Art Press**, now an imprint of **Karen Mireau Books.** To date, she has published over 100 diverse titles—including novels, poetry, picture books, middle grade and young adult fiction, and numerous memoirs.

It's been her bliss ever since—but she has never abandoned her love for the natural world. She continues to plant gardens of nurturing food, flowers, and medicinal plants wherever she lives.

Karen now calls the wine country of Sonoma, California, home. Alongside her husband, photographer Raymond Rimmer, she continues to write, garden, paint, publish, and shower her friends, family, and grandchildren with unending affection and love.

Other Titles of Interest
by Karen Mireau

All Their Yesterdays
Novel, 2019.

The Architect of Fire
Poems, 2024.

The Conscientious Visitor
Karen Mireau
& Marla Lay
Nonfiction, 2013.

The Cottage Hotel: The History & Untold Tales of Mendon Hamlet's Legendary Tavern and Stagecoach Inn
Anthology, 2023.

The Cottage Hotel Songbook
Lyrics & Music, 2023.

Cracker Jack-Jack
Karen Mireau
& Zoey Williams
Picture Book, 2021.

Ever After : An Artist's Childhood
Karen Mireau
& Cynthia Garlock Kozlowski
Memoir, 2018.

Front Porch Lessons: The Stories of Alma & George Johnson
Memoir, 2024.

Marienau : A Daughter's Reflections
Karen Mireau
& Dr. Annemarie Roeper
Memoir, 2012.

Matsu.Kaze : The Wind in the Pines
Poems, 2016.

Oh No! Emma!
Picture Book, 2018.

Redfield Place
Poems, 2021.

Sweet Land of Liberty : 50 Years Later
Karen Mireau
& John Wedda
Illustrated book on civil rights, 2015.

Sycamore Road
Poems, 2024.

Tell Me Again |
That the Dead Do Dream
Poems, 2024.

Two Thousand Rains
Poems, 2024.

Karen the "Entre-manure"
in her happy place
on Satori Permaculture Farm | 2000

To Contact the Author
please email:
KarenMireauBooks@gmail.com

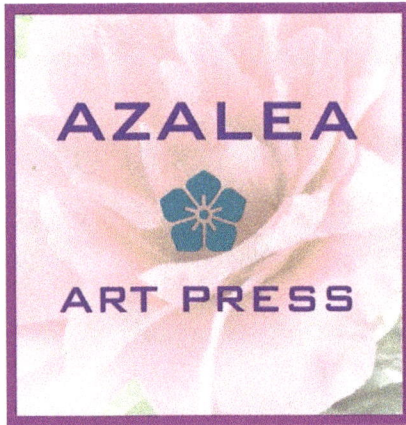

AZALEA

ART PRESS

For Direct Book Orders
please visit
www.Lulu.com

To learn more:
https://karenmireaubooks.com